carmen TAFOLLa
new anD selecTeD poems

Books by Carmen Tafolla

Poetry:
Get Your Tortillas Together (coauthored with Reyes Cárdenas and
    Cecilio García-Camarillo)
Curandera
"La Isabela de Guadalupe y El Apache Mio Cid" (in *Five Poets of Aztlan*)
Sonnets to Human Beings/Sonnette An Menschen
Sonnets to Human Beings & Other Selected Works
Sonnets & Salsa
Rebozos
This River Here: Poems of San Antonio

Short Story Collections:
The Holy Tortilla and a Pot of Beans: A Feast of Short Fiction

Nonfiction:
To Split a Human: Mitos, Machos, y La Mujer Chicana
Tamales, Comadres & The Meaning of Civilization
Latinos: Great Lives From History, Vols. 1-3 (edited with Martha Cotera)
A Life Crossing Borders: Memoir of a Mexican-American Confederate

Children's Books:
The Dog Who Wanted to Be a Tiger
My House is Your House
Baby Coyote & The Old Woman/El Coyotito y La Viejita
El Día que el Armadillo Vió su Sombra
*That's Not Fair: Emma Tenayuca's Fight for Justice/No Es Justo!La Lucha
    de Emma Tenayuca por la Justicia* (coauthored with Sharyll Teneyuca)
Somebody Stole My Smile
What Can You DO with a Rebozo?
What Can you DO with a Paleta?
Fiesta Babies
I'll Always Come Back to You

carmen tafolla
new and selected poems

TCU press
Fort worth, texas

TCU Texas poet Laureate series

Library of Congress Cataloging-in-Publication Data

Names: Tafolla, Carmen, 1951- author.
Title: New and selected poems / Carmen Tafolla.
Other titles: TCU Texas poets laureate series.
Description: Fort Worth, Texas : TCU Press, [2018] | Series: TCU Texas poet
   laureate series | In English, some poems in Spanish.
Identifiers: LCCN 2018010260 | ISBN 9780875656892 (alk. paper)
Subjects: LCSH: American poetry--Mexican American authors. | LCGFT: Poetry.
Classification: LCC PS3570.A255 A6 2018 | DDC 811/.54--dc23
LC record available at https://urldefense.proofpoint.com/v2/url?u=https-3A__lccn.loc.gov_2018010260&d=DwIFAg&c=7Q-FWLBTAxn3T_E3HWrz-GYJrC4RvUoWDrzTlitGRH_A&r=O2eiy819IcwTGuw-vrBGiVdmhQxMh2yx eggw9qlTUDE&m=t7T89donom8ncxtgWUzDyqL6Xo3hUvGIrVKl8m388 MQ&s=g0N7bkoYaPt9v16Xqwfggplwkhmr1ok77dcsQymRa-A&e=

TCU Press
TCU Box 298300
Fort Worth, TX 76129
817.257.7822
www.prs.tcu.edu

To order books: 1.800.826.8911

Designed by fusion29
www.fusion29.com

TO THE ONE WHO BRUNG ME,
AND THE ONE I ALWAYS DANCE WITH,
MUCH GRATITUDE AND, AS ALWAYS, TODO MI AMOR, TO
ERNESTO MARROQUÍN BERNAL.
POR TI VOLARÉ, Y BAILARÉ.

15

contents

INTRODUCTION

Carmen Tafolla's roots in San Antonio literally predate the founding of the city, so it was fitting that she was selected as the city's first-ever Poet Laureate. San Antonio is unique among Texas cities in having created a position with considerable funding behind it, but even so, they had no idea what a dynamo they had set in motion by selecting Carmen. During her two-year tenure, a period during which she battled chemotherapy, radiation, and surgery for breast cancer, she created, sponsored, and participated in some three hundred poetry-related events and activities, mostly benefitting San Antonio's least-served communities. Simultaneously, one of her early books of poetry, *Curandera*, had the honor of being one of the multicultural titles banned in Arizona. *Librotraficantes* began almost immediately "smuggling" copies of *Curandera* into the state to be given away to students. Always something of a legend, Carmen became even more renowned with each presentation and reading. *Curandera*, first published in 1983 and now available in a thirtieth anniversary edition, was called in Dr. Norma E. Cantú's introduction "a love song, for . . . the healing energy of the words . . . to carry you into that place of dreams where poems live."

In 2015, Carmen was named the Texas State Poet Laureate, only the second Chicana/Latina to hold that position. That position, while unfunded, provided a new level of access to Carmen's work. She single-handedly raised enough money to fund an extended tour of schools, teaching workshops and celebrating poetry in many of the state's poorest school districts.

So, where did this one-woman *fuerza de la naturaleza* come from? Carmen Mary Tafolla was born on July 29, 1951, in San Antonio. She grew up in the Westside neighborhood known as Barrio de la Tripa. The Tafolla side of the family had lived in San Antonio since the 1850s, but her great-grandmother Salinas connected Carmen to the very beginnings of San Antonio. One of her forebears—actually her great-great-great-great-great grandfather—was Domingo Flores de Abrego, a soldier who helped build the original presidio over a decade before the "first" civilian settlers from the Canary Islands arrived in San Antonio in 1731. In 1719, Domingo and his wife, Manuela Treviño, had a child, Pedro Flores de Abrego, one of the very first Spanish-Mexican children to be born in what would soon become San Antonio de Béxar. The history of the Tafolla family in the Americas goes back even further. The first Tafolla documented to have been born on this side of the Atlantic was Juan de Tafoya Altamirano de Estrada (b. 1640 in Real de Minas de Tlalpujahua, Michoacán). By 1661 he was living in Santa Cruz, in what is now New Mexico. His great-grandson, General Phelipe Tafoya, was the Alcalde of Santa Fe, New Mexico in the 1770s. Phelipe's great-grandson was Santiago Tafolla Sr., born in 1837, who brought the family name to San Antonio when he moved here in the 1850s. Santiago Sr. was a writer, and his memoir of his life as a scout, Indian fighter, US camel-keeper, Confederate soldier, and Methodist minister, and as a victim of racism, is one of the most important documents of its era. Translated and edited by Carmen and her cousin, Laura Tafolla, it was published as *A Life Crossing Borders*. One of Santiago's sons, Santiago Jr.—Carmen's great uncle—was an early activist, and was among the founders of the School Improvement League, the Cruz Azul Mexicano, Order of the Sons of America, and other Mexican American organizations in the 1920s and '30s.

Visitors to San Antonio in the nineteenth century routinely praised the city for its environs and its multilingual and cosmopolitan atmosphere, but by the time Carmen was growing up in the 1950s, racism had divided the city. Many Westside streets were unpaved; there were no public libraries there; schools were underfunded, overcrowded, and ruled by strict anti-Spanish laws with severe punishments. Mexican Americans were definitely second-class citizens. A long struggle for equality under the law was just beginning in America, and Carmen Tafolla and her poetry would be a part of that struggle.

Growing up on the Westside was not easy for a young Chicana, but apparently Carmen's commitment to community improvement began early. We find a photograph of Carmen—at four years old—on the front page of the *San Antonio Light* newspaper, measuring the depth of a pothole with a yardstick! At Ivanhoe Elementary School, Carmen recalls that there were "no clubs, no library, no student opportunities." In middle school, she won the school spelling bee two years in a row, although the chief skill she learned was probably survival. Rhodes Middle School was reputedly the "roughest school on the Westside," where students were frisked daily. She memorialized it as such in her poem, "When I Dream Dreams."

Keystone School, a private school for gifted students on the "nicer" side of town, briefly offered full scholarships to the highest scorers on a general intelligence testing to which students from all sides of the city were invited. Carmen was one of the recipients of Keystone's largesse. Initially, Keystone was a difficult transition culturally, and she was definitely a "fish out of water," but she excelled, and was awarded scholarships to Texas Lutheran College in Seguin and Austin College in Sherman, Texas, where she earned her BA and MA degrees. Carmen received her PhD in Bilingual and Foreign Language Education from the University of Texas in 1982.

In 1973, Carmen became the first Chicana faculty member to direct a Chicano Studies Center in the United States, at Texas Lutheran College in Seguin. She was also the head writer for *Sonrisas*, a pioneering bilingual television show for children. By 1975, the *movimiento Chicano* was in full flower, and Carmen was publishing poetry in Chicano literary magazines like *Caracol*. Her first book was published in 1976. *Get Your Tortillas Together* was a collaboration with two other South Texas poets, Reyes Cardenas and Cecilio García-Camarillo.

During this time Carmen began to develop her talents for dramatic readings, and she presented her poems at the historic National Chicano literary gatherings called *Floricantos*, starting with her reading at *Floricanto Dos* in Austin in March 1975. The Chicano movement in the 1970s was still male dominated, and women had difficulty not only being published, but even being included in readings and programs. M&A Editions, a Texas Chicano micro-press run by poet Angela De Hoyos and her husband, Moises Sandoval, helped to break down the gender divide. Carmen's first full-length collection of poetry, *Curandera*, came out in 1983 from M&A Editions. As Carmen said later, "I wanted to focus on la pachuquita, la viejita, la madre, la curandera, la rebelde, on full, living, breathing females." *Curandera* did just that.

Curandera filled a cultural and linguistic void. The author applied a poet's eye and a scholar's mind to employing the natural Spanish and English code-switching of her Westside San Antonio barrio as a literary language, not unlike great poets of the past—Chaucer among them, to whom she alludes in her poem "Right in One Language"—who shaped their own languages through innovative multilingual poetics. Carmen has long been regarded as one of the masters of this type of poetic code-switching, and *Curandera* is considered by scholars to be a core document in this regard.

The year after *Curandera* was published, Carmen's first nonfiction book appeared, *To Split a Human: Mitos, Machos, y la Mujer Chicana*, one of the earliest Chicana books to address directly the racism-sexism dynamic.

Many other books followed: poetry, collections of short fiction, books for young children and young adults. But poetry has always been at the center of Carmen's writing. Her *Sonnets to Human Beings and Other Selected Works* included not only the title selection (winner of the First Prize in Poetry for the University of California at Irvine's 1989 National Chicano Literature Contest) and other poems and short stories, but also several essays on Tafolla and her work. It is thought to be the first critical edition published on any Chicano/a writer, and includes many of the pieces that shaped the basis of Tafolla's one-woman show, *My Heart Speaks a Different Language* (a.k.a. *Las Voces de mi Gente* and *Las Voces de San Antonio*), which she has performed in Europe, Canada, New Zealand, and Latin America. Carmen developed a new performance of indigenous women's voices, derived from a more recent collection of ekphrastic poems, *Rebozos*. She also published a collection of poems heavily based on the voices and the experiences of South Texas, the widely praised *Sonnets and Salsa*, and a collection of poetry of place, also about San Antonio, *This River Here*.

Carmen is the author of several award-winning books for children and young adults, including *The Holy Tortilla and a Pot of Beans: A Feast of Short Fiction*, *That's Not Fair! Emma Tenayuca's Struggle for Justice / ¡No Es Justo! La lucha de Emma Tenayuca por la justicia* (written with Sharyll Teneyuca), *Baby Coyote and the Old Woman / El Coyotito y la Viejita*, *Fiesta Babies*, *What Can You DO With A Rebozo?*, and *What Can You DO With A Paleta?* Her children's and young adult titles have earned prestigious awards such as the Charlotte Zolotow Award for best children's picture book writing (she was the first Latina to be so honored); the Américas Award, presented at the Library of Congress; two Tomás Rivera Book Awards; three ALA Notable Book listings; and five International Latino Book Awards. Two of the honors she values most were given to her in her hometown. In 1999, St. Mary's University presented her with its Art of Peace Award for writings that contribute to "peace, justice, and human understanding." In 2017, she was presented with the city's Distinction in the Arts award. She was not the first Chicana to be elected a member of the Texas Institute of Letters, but as of March 2018, she will become its first Chicana President.

Carmen Tafolla has held a variety of faculty and administrative posts at universities throughout the Southwest. She has been a freelance educational consultant on bilingual education, writing and creativity, and cultural diversity issues for almost four decades, and founded and briefly directed a school for gifted and creative children. Currently she is professor of transformative children's literature at the University of Texas at San Antonio.

The National Association for Chicano Studies recognized Carmen for "work that gives voice to the peoples and cultures of this land"; the author of *Roots*, Alex Haley, called her "a world class writer"; Ana Castillo called her a "pioneer of Chicana literature." She is among the most anthologized of all Latina writers, and has performed her poetry all over the world. But wherever she has gone, Carmen has always called San Antonio home, and her poetry and stories have always celebrated the city and its distinctive *cultura*.

In the current volume, we hear in Carmen's newer poems a voice coping with the vicissitudes of life, both personal and affecting the world at large. The death of her mother at age ninety-nine, the loss of her beloved husband, Ernesto Bernal, the struggle against breast cancer, the suffering of the planet itself all enter into these new poems. And yet, what must we do while "awaiting the Angel of Death"? We write, she says, with "*plumas* only we still remember how to use"; we watch, she tells us, for "one drop of stubborn sunlight / one ungestapoed heartful of dirt" in which we must plant the seeds of "resistance / change / love."

In *This River Here: Poems of San Antonio*, she advises us all to be "story-keepers," to really look, to really listen, to really remember, because she writes, "This is how / we keep our history. / This is how / we keep our souls."

Bryce Milligan
San Antonio, Texas
2017

I

New Poems

even the scars...

are not unaffected
their permanence softened
to the challenge of yet
another day

After thirty years
most of the corners
of my life have the taste of you
somewhere
in the air
around the edges of their vowels,
shapes of their consonants, continents,
dreams   one of us dreamed, the other told
both forgot which one   it was,
the way the mattress curves into place
without being asked, the way my hand
follows your shoulder down the stairs,
a better banister for balance
in the avalanche of life

Everything melted, molded, softened
to the challenge of another world
of new, or shocking, sharp
or still recognizable
corners

yes, even the scars
change, soften, stretch
and curve to fit
together

Altar to the Dead

-Dia de los Muertos 2015

We dance with the dead
we serve them at our kitchen table
We dance with the dead
we serenade them on our knees
We smash the piñata of time
with fiesta-colored broomsticks
and know Los Muertos are forever with us
woven into our veins, our dreams
We dance with the dead
twirl them in una polka sabrosita,
share their bread, pour out our lungs in song
spend a day with them breathing in our arms
spend a night with them floating beyond the pull of life
beyond the superficial semblance of death
beyond the flesh, beyond the mind
our souls awake to the infinite power
of laughing Spirit
Creator, Destroyer, Transformer
Love more relevant than
a simple borderline between
life and death

a spirit in me

Sip slowly, or life will undo you.
Sip cautiously, wary of snake venom,
sensing for cactus thorn, fish spine, scorpion juice.
Sip gratefully, aware how very much each day
hauls in on bounteous shoulders just returned
from jungles long outliving civilizations.
Sip with eyes wide open, the whole soul alert
and breathless, drenched hungrily
in the color of clean, savage dawn

Approach cautiously, this moment of encounter
for there is a spirit in me
wild, not born of words,
not conceived of flesh
nor bound by the parameters of *pueblos*.
This spirit, born of blood-scream sunburst,
tantalizingly *delicious*, awaits the attack
Dripping blood like *baba,* from the corners of a smile
still grinding raw sustenance over hungry teeth
still drunk with birth and squint-eyed survival

OJO! Beware the danger, for there is a spirit in me
that consumes. Devours, explodes, and germinates.
This Mayan Ix, Nahua Teyollocuani, Tex-Mex Soul-Swallowing Me
shape-shifts between each magic second
invisible to your dumbstruck eyes
but pulsing from your veins, *pounding* now,
born from earthen heart beating under tangled jungle floor
keeping me, and you, and histories
alive, gasping gulps of breath of corn
of quenching rain, of eucalyptus trees
of pyramid rhythms more advanced than relativity
Listen. Hear the drumbeats just beyond the village

Feel the surging vines wrapping your legs
the sharp dizzying conciencia rushing blood
behind your eyes, improving vision
sinew rippling in anticipation
of the transformation
My Mayan heart consumes me, open,
dispersing to the wind the seeds of unbound,
stubborn, universal *life*.

Beware, for there is a spirit in you
that is wild and not born of words
keeping you and me and histories
alive
and pounding
deep and echoed power
from underneath
this jungle floor

sanity, repossessed

Deep in this spreading dust-filled desert
laid forgetfully in Nowhere, Mexico
Sunthawed skies
gentle the bite of winter
Cacti lose their thorns
grow lush like shade trees

Abandoned railroad cars
tossed off the track like paper cups
bow as families introduce themselves as
relatives and move in shyly,
adopting hard rust walls
and rough industrial floors
Mothers plant gardens of eager chayotes,
spread sarapes like stylish curtains
across the open door

Mornings are cool
Acceptance sips wisdom
prays give us our daily bread
and an occasional cactus tuna
Purple-ripe prickly pear juice
drips down a grateful chin like honey
and the technologically-bred tropical desert
blooms
a smiling green
survival

IT was so COLD

the day that mud fell from the sky.
So unearthly a chill cracked our bones
from the inside, tremoring its way out
like a windshield shattering its way to doom.
It was the same spring that everyone's
winter cough wouldn't go away
hacking our throats, hijacking our lungs.
No one knew what it was.
The rich complained that the handyman hadn't
washed the car well enough the day before.
The working class grumbled that
the drive-thru carwash
hadn't lasted even a day
before this messy rain got to it—
it WAS rain, wasn't it?
The poor didn't notice much difference
on their cars (or buses)
the dirty splotches just a tiny bit
more dirty.
And the poets noticed only
that the windows they stared out—
were covered with a quiet grey crust,
smeared further by those prosaically odd drops
that came from the sky that day.

It was as if no one noticed at all
that it wasn't the mud,
the dirt, the inconvenience, the ashen dinginess
leaving us vulnerable.
It wasn't the stubborn virus, resistant strain,
the factory fumes, the allergies, the stress.

It was the earth
the earth herself
Feverish seizures, fluids

finally leaking forth.
The phlegm, the vomit,
pus and blood
in their first stage
of draining out

A quick expulsion
unplanned elimination
from her over-ravaged,
over-poisoned,
over-disrespected
dying body

which no one would think
to bathe or gently wrap
or hold in wake
or grieve

sometimes, age

Sometimes Age creeps stealthily into the house
Intruder, when everyone is in the backyard
laughing over the barbeque grill
planning exotic vacations
or delightful pregnancies
Stowaway in the attic
living a life undetected
Even as he steals the bread from our pantry
at midnight
the telomeres from our DNA
at birthdays
A secret covered in the dust
of old photo albums
his existence quiet as the termites
patient as flea eggs in rat feces
hopeful as the unwound alarm clock
in the Samsonite suitcase
knowing that, sooner or later,
he will be
discovered

LOSING YOU

one piece at a time
my breath shallow, stiff
as a perfect red balloon
filled with helium and
framed by sun's rays,
ascends into heaven
from some distant parking lot
I do not recognize

the lilt of a song disappears
a word lost here, a memory there
first, you can't sing, or do stairs,
two-step calculations, drive
cannot finish the
sentence
walk
but

your love
still clear as crystal
sparkles through the greyblack clouds
you smile
brave
strong
still every bit the man you always
were

my breath catches in my throat
a pinprick of *Destino*
I wonder if the helium
is whispering out
one invisible drip of
life at a time

the beautiful red globe
floats off into the distant sky
exploring exotic places
to which I
no longer
have access

REVISION

—2004

I am growing closer to my skeleton
on more acquainted terms with my death
I am dipping playful toes in those
murky waters of a river border
which I might be tempted to—yes,
cross, illegally, just for a while,
indocumentada, sin papeles,
just *un capricho, un antojito*
just to visit, *convivir,*
old family, friends,
living on the other side

I am growing closer to my skeleton
each day seeing possibilities
wondering who will go first
who will cross over splashing loudly,
clanking femur and humerus together,
clavicle and scapula tinkling thinly

I realize the risks
feel the deep currents
receding undertows
but still I watch these waters,
river fluid and of variable route
Dip in toes, withdraw,
Consider just a trip,
Stay away

I am growing closer to my skeleton
Expressing from below the flesh

intimate with etheric features
See me now
Each day a bone closer
to my final
face

THIS IS a PLace

This is a place
that doesn't fit easily
inside the tight bindings
of a definition
doesn't sit comfortably
within the prescribed boundaries
spills over flags and rivers,
borders, barbed wire fences
defying everything
it's said to be.
Sleet falls from the hot, mid-May sky
so uncannily cold it still huddles frozen
in the driveway two hours later.
That August we're declared
a disaster area for drought
declared again, four weeks later,
a disaster area for flood.
The tornado rips the roof
off our garage, doesn't touch a flower
on the neighbor's mimosa tree.
This is a place
that doesn't fit the expectations.

This is a place
that sounds as if
it doesn't really exist.
Animals thought impossible survive and
thrive in body, or legend. Jaguarundis
have dog eyes and cat faces. Chupacabras
suck the blood of life then disappear to live
beyond the pale, coexisting without violence
to those big birds with human features that
only occasionally swoop down to scandalize
human towns. Horny toads, lightning bugs,

armadillos, wild javelinas that trample what they don't
eat. Coyotes break their bonds with canines and turn
vegetarian. Or whatever it takes to
survive.

This is a place that, like some strange Australia,
preserves so many marsupial unknowns, things with
pockets, or hidden caverns, secret histories, petroglyphs
with codes we no longer understand.
Where even at the missions three hundred years
ago, the priests and captains may have had the wax-sealed
paper of the law, but did not control what went on
in a city renamed for their Saints,
where Coahuiltecans carried on as they
had for centuries, traded, buried, loved, and lived
and built a town of sabor and shade
upon the indomitable patchwork colcha
of bluebonnets and buffalo grass.

This is a place where the abundance of water or sun,
vegetation or cattle, tourist or developer,
can only sit like a silent spectator
to the massiveness of spirit
and the giant hand of time carved into
canyons, rivers, ocean-bed deserts, and
footprints of dinosaurs a gentle drive away
from spaceships that travel to the moon
and always
always
back. For
this is a place
worth
the coming
back.

SOMETHING SEVERED
—2013

when the sharp-billed hawk cuts its knifepath
through the tender sky, shears the infant mouse
from its screeching grieving mother, something
in the deep heart of the sky flashes like sickened
green lightning, a sign of a storm not expected, not
suited to the summer's wardrobe of warm melodies

a coyote finds itself voiceless, searching for its howl
a trembling tree stripped, missing its own broad shade
and my hand—abruptly encountering this scarred hole
in a beating chest, this hardwalled cave, carved deep
and ragged, where once there rose a soft hill of breast

Now pacing paws and chanting drumwood,
I howl out the thunder's song
visioning, repaint the color of the lightning
growing green vocal cords, re-sing the history of bark
claim the cool shade remembered, where
I listen, hear the earth softwhisper,
    Soy tu Madre, M'ija,
This is less than whisper, more than breath
in her maternal lullaby. A whistle of a wind seems to sigh,
    El Tiempo cambia todo, changes, takes away, returns
    Knifepaths and Storms are small, cosa chiquita,
    just something severed, something gained
    while this, my planet, spins and spins
    turns to the moon and then away
    Your face ever changing,
    your form, the shaman of a jaguar,
    grandmother of a tree
    El horizonte mas tranquilo hums in harmony
    pulls you into the passage choir of voices
    a moving, melting swirl of stars
    in its own universe,
    the sum unchanged, M'ija

WHERE MY FATHER BUILT HIS HOUSE

Where my father built his house
the dirt color *canela* seeps like cinnamon bark
a healing tea to warm the body gently into life

Where my father built his house
the wind draws each breath deep and rhythmic
a workman drawing each blow full, to make the next

Where my father built his house
the wood slow-ages into strength,
tree or table, stool or chair, things meant to last
longer than the lives of those who built them
Stories meant to be cradled
songs intended to be heard

inside the weave of the fabric, the rub of the wood,
the stone of the wall, the warp of the bone
things meant to go on. An echoed memory
of how much work
went into the life
we were given permission to live

Where my father built his house
mesquite blocks of stubborn history
pave the paths
sing with the coo of ageless doves
shine, a sun's kiss on the dewleaves of dawn
polish the prints on our fingertips, palms, hearts

till old *injusticias* back off, into the soil,
embarrassed. Ancient pathways erode,
transform, remake, reguide, inspire

while *testigos* of hope, sweat, and desperate *milagros*
tip their respectful hats and whisper
like stubborn, undying ghosts their promise

to carry on
to carry on
to carry on

GЄNTLY APART

The stars burn thinly now
pierce holes into the sky
as we watch the world
fall gently apart

The pretend corn will not make seed
and the kernels coerced
under a steel microscope
will never germinate or bloom
into new greenness from the raped earth.

The planet herself has been
torn from her organs
Womb and lungs and colon bleeding
into each other as the violator curses,
under his money-drunk breath,
Frack You!

We pretend it is still good to breathe
the red-dusted air and drink
the grey-white water, nibble on
the perfectly-shaped plastic corn,
pretend that the earth will grow on
tomorrow and tomorrow and tomorrow
as baseball-sized hail bombards Texas
in May
in the middle of a heat streak.

The president pretends to follow the law
and the representatives pretend
to listen to the people
and the farmers pretend
to grow real food
while universities pretend to teach
what students
pretend
to learn

WHAT TO DO WHILE AWAITING THE ANGEL OF DEATH, OR, THE ANGEL OF LIFE

Plant softly. Majestically. And always,
con respeto. Y amor. Seeds are our children
from a different mother. Nights are our
Angels, restoring pools of rest and planning
Even in times when we hide, secret blood painted
on our doors with brushes only we can see, with
plumas only we still remember how to use, even then
the Angels still remember how to find us, huddled,
shivering, praying, breathing in our dreams for dawn,
sueños del amanecer, sueños de la libertad,
squeezing all the seeds we can, in each palm
awaiting just one drop of stubborn sunlight
one ungestapoed heartful of dirt
one action brave enough
to grow
    resistance
    change
    love

II

Poems from *Curandera* (1983)
and
Get Your Tortillas Together (1976)

AQUÍ

He wanders through the crooked streets
that mimic river beds Before
and breathes the anxious air in traffic
filled with tension left from wooded crossroads in attack
He shops the Windows, happy,
where the stalking once was good
and his kitchen floor is built on bones
of venison once gently roasted.

"It's a good place for a party!" he concurs
to friends now dressed in jeans.

The ground was already beaten smooth
and festive by the joy of ancient dances.

He feels the warmth,
and doesn't know his soul is filled
with the spirit of coyotes past.

Y CUANDO PIENSO EN TÍ

y cuando pienso en tí . . .
pienso en las olas de mares secretos
que jamás han conocido ni mentiras ni dominación
que broncas nacen y broncas bailan
y broncas viven su exaltación.

pienso en las rocas bruñidas, alisadas,
esculpidas por los siglos con la marca de amor,
de la pared mas alta del castillo mas viejo
en el valle lozano de mi corazón.

pienso en las jarras enterradas, vidriadas,
que, sencillas, sobreviven dueño, duelo, y civilización.
que en su obra, dan vida, y en su vida, dan gracia,
que refrescan, y cargan agua, cuento, y canción.

pienso en tus ojos, antorchas encendidas,
que regalan miradas, caminos, y calor.
pienso en planetas de lunas gemelas
de tierras perladas de raro valor.
de seres valientes de ojos danzantes
que sueñan y cambian su gema color.

pienso en tu alma de calor y coraje
ardor y justicia, viveza y amor.
pienso en cristales de eternal pureza,
diamantes ardientes de espontánea belleza
adornando cavernas de primordial creación
adornando el universo con su paz y pasión.

pienso en lo siempre de un manantial
brotando melodías y gozo y frenesí.
pienso en un viento de vida-aire sinigual
y en un eterno querer cuando pienso en tí
un eterno querer, cuando pienso en tí.

voyage

I was the fourth ship.
    Behind Niña, Pinta, Santa María,
    Lost at sea while watching a seagull,
    Following the wind and sunset skies,
    While the others set their charts.

I was the fourth ship.
    Breathing in salt and flying with clouds,
    Sailing moonbreezes and starvision nights,
    Rolling into the wave and savoring its lull,
    While the others pointed their prows.

I was the fourth ship.
    Playfully in love with the sea,
    Eternally entwined with the sky,
    Forever vowed to my voyage,
    While the others shouted "Land."

ALLÍ POR LA CALLE SAN LUIS

West Side—corn tortillas for a penny each
  Made by an ancient woman
    and her mother.
  Cooked on the homeblack of a flat stove,
  Flipped to slap the birth awake,
  Wrapped by corn hands.
Toasted morning light and dancing history—
  earth gives birth to corn gives birth to man
  gives birth to earth.
Corn tortillas—penny each.
  No tax.

san antonio

They called you lazy
They saw your silent subtle screaming eyes
And called you lazy
They saw your lean, bronzed workmaid's arms
And called you lazy
They saw your centuries-secret sweet-night song
And called you lazy

San Antonio,
They saw your skybirth and sunaltar
Your corndirt soul and mute bell toll
Your river ripple heart, soft with life
Your ancient shawl of sigh on strife
And didn't see

San Antonio,
They called you lazy

III

Poems from *Sonnets to Human Beings*
and Other Selected Works (1992)

HOW SHALL I TELL YOU?

*After listening to the world news, the verge of war, the firing of
warships in the Persian Gulf, international crisis after interna-
tional crisis, and wondering whether, in the morning, we would
still be here, any of us . . .*

When no soul walks the softened green
and no foot beats the pulse on crumbling brown
and no one lives to sing to rain
or soak to sun the spirit of its golden gown
to weave the many colors of the after-arch
from sky to human skin to wooded wealth
in fiber fabrics beads and tusks and seeds
all leading up in rows of beauty drumbeat to black
        neck, like venison in stealth

When no one lulls the child to sleep
or takes the wrinkled story's hand
or listens to the news—a wired sound
of tribe on tribe and—stet now—man on man
how shall I tell you that I love you then?
How shall I touch your fingers tip to tip
    and say that we were blood and human voice and friend?

THE MAGIC

—to the child in the photo (and all the others)

Such magic in a child there is, such life,
Such fountainburst of days and love and hope
The magic breath of tiny hands and heart
That beat and breathe and suffer try, and cope.
But ribs, like tree roots arching to the skies,
Face upward, caking o'er the ground so dry,
And hunger curls the spine, affronts our eyes:
You will not live. And yet, you will not die.

The love that ripened in your first wet cry,
The hope that sheltered you when arms could not
Will not retreat nor silent keep their sigh:
In naked truth they lash our superficial lies
    (like war and wealth and coldness comfort-taught)
Your eyes now frozen in the lens and paper flat
    Give hope that our hearts cold might yet survive.
For this, you will not know but grace, and, dove,
In truth as death, you will not be but love.

POQUITO ALLÁ

This hand?
This hand, he says,
It was an accident.
You do not understand
Poquito aquí, Poquito allá,
that's how Dios meant it, *ves*, to be.
It doesn't bother me too much
In fact, it gives me less to work about.
Less people who will trust their broken chairs to me.
Yet I can still these roses plant
like that one standing by your feet
Las Siete Hermanas, for they always bloom together
like sweet sisters, seven in each bunch.
and I can still make *chocolate*, stirring strong,
the fingers do not slow me down
these two, nor this one sewed back on.

It's funny, don't you think,
how in those many years at Kelly Field
or even in the war, Dios solo sabe, so many
around me dead, or legs or arms just floating off to sea
but I came back—it must have been my mother's prayers—
the only thing the worse for it my teeth.
The Navy took us perfect, sent us back a mess.
And yet, I had so much
aún every limb and digit there
my whole life full
and so I can't complain.
This hand still does so much
for me—why just today
I planted ten small seeds
—cilantro for Mamá,
that woman loves it even in her beans—
and pressed the earth down on them soft
like her soft fingers when she caresses me.

And picked the eggs out for my sisters
y sus nietos. They taste different fresh
like this, las de las tiendas no comparan.

Oh but you want to know what happened?
Well, it's not too bad, nomás que
Chuy's neighbor still won't talk to me
goes way around the grocery store
when he runs into me
I guess he's scared to see.
Some people, sometimes, son así.
Se siente mal, because he was the one who said,
Reach down in there for me and git that wrench,
And then he flipped the switch too soon
Ya casi era tiempo de salir
I'd worked for him all day and he
was eager to pay up, clean up, go home
and didn't wait to see that it was out.
Así, se acabó.
The doctors sewed this one back on
aunque los que no están
molestan menos que este aquí.

Too bad it bothers him so much.
I still do all I used to 'cept for
playing the guitar and carving wood.
The rest I do just fine, tho' maybe not as good.
Y el pobre always was uncomfortable with Mexicans
Y ahora peor.
Forgot to pay me for that day
or maybe scared to send the cash
for fear I'd ask for more.
Well, that's okay, this hand still knows
to *saludar*, shake hands, y abrazar
and only yesterday, my baby grandson stood right up
solito, holding on to these good fingers here.
Derecho, fuerte, unafraid.
Poquito aquí, poquito allá.

RIGHT IN ONE LANGUAGE

Write in one language, they say,
and agents sit and glare hairy brows
over foreign words and, almost trying hope,
say, *It's not French, is it?*

But it isn't.
Nor is my mind
when I try tight, clean line
manicured to be like Leave
It to Beaver's house
       straight sidewalk
       so square hedges
       and if there's one on
this   side there's also one on   that
Equally paced
       placed
       spaced
       controlled

You seem to lose control of the line
in this one, he says, *it all explodes.*
  I see bilingue-beautiful
     explosions
        two worlds collide
           two tongues dance
              inside the cheek
                together
Por aquí poquito   and a dash allá también
Salsa   chacha   disco polka
Rock that Texan cumbia
in a molcajete mezcla!

But restrain yourself,
The Man pleads sanity,
Trim the excess
just enough and nothing more

Think Shaker room and lots of light
two windows, Puritan-clean floors and chairs
up on simple pegs, three.
y las palabritas mías
    are straining at the yoke
two-headed sunflowers
peeking through St. Moderatius grass
waiting for familias grandes
garden growing wild
with Mexican hierbitas, spices, rosas,
baby trees nurtured así, muy natural
    No one knows yet
    if they're two years old
    and should be weaned
    or pruned
    or toilet trained
    but they are given only
    agua y cariñitos
    shade and sun and companía
City Inspection Crew
House and Gardens Crew
Publication Crew agree
the lack of discipline
lack of Puritan
        purity
          pior y tí.

Chaucer must have felt like this,
the old Pachuco playing his TexMex onto the page
and even then, the critics said,

        Write
        in one language.
But when he pondered all that cleanness, so controlled,
forms halved, he just could not deny
his own familia, primos from both sides
    weeds that liked to crawl
    over sidewalks pa' juntarse
    visit, stretch out comfy

natural and lusty
hybrid wealth
and told them it was just because
he was undisciplined
unpolished
and did not know
how to make love
with just
one
person
in the room
or
on the page

And he, like me,
did what he wanted anyway
But you, like they,
want Shaker hallways
while I grow Mexican gardens
and weed-rich backyards
There are 2 many colors in the marketplace
to play modest, when Mexico and
Gloria Rodríguez both say,
Estos gringos con su Match-Match
y a mí me gusta Mix-Mix!
There are 2 many cariños to be created
to stay within the lines
2 many times
when I want to tell you
There is room
here
for two
tongues
inside this
kiss.

NO TIENES LÍMITES

a slice of you
does not fit on paper
  (unless one wears
   glasses ground with filters
   for the sun)

a slice of you
bursts with pleasure
in the mouth
can only be tasted
at midnight
when ink cannot testify
math cannot measure
and time and consciousness
are turned off
so humans can exist
without limitations

where go those things

where go those things
that were said to us
and not heard
where go those words
that were almost whispered
from the thirsty tongue
cracked grey with crust of death
where go those messages
the mouth could not quite form
shaped around a groan
and we could not make out
but we saw the rolling eyes
and heard the tone
untold

where go those things
that were said to us?
In the morning
the body is placed in the ground
the flutter of the eyes
still echoing in my mind
and by evening,
soft raindrops resting sentry,
the swallows have returned home
to the earth-bricked Mission.

walking the dreampoem

I too have been stripped clean to the bone
growing silent amid the cries of the unbarked
left unsheathed in honesty
cracking with the give of the wood of past generations
and aging with the memory of their voices.

I too have been taken to the earthfire
camped on my own essence and my own entrails
bowed, aching, scorched
and have shorn my leaves windlessly
living mouth-to-mouth with the breath of breaking.

I too have been bent to the wind
rubbed naked in its wake
scarred through seven years' rings
and dying many times alone.

Yet so, between the forest of the birch
and the birches in their fall
your chant surfaces
dark and squirming newborn
through the echo of the years,
still trying to be helpless

But the mountains have grown strong surrounding me
I am different now
The spirits are too clear
to be washed away by rain
or hidden by lush leaves.

I too have been stripped clean to the bark,
growing silent among the cries of the unborn,
left suckling raw sap of acceptance and wonder
alongside the orphaned, the displaced, the stranger.

But the wood of my chest has grown and aged in tune,
in time, fully to its natural bent
and the twigs decide whether to break under me
as I go walking the dreampoem through the present.

marked

Never write with pencil,
m'ija.
It is for those
who would
erase.
Make your mark proud
    and open,
Brave,
       beauty folded into
  its imperfection,
Like a piece of turquoise
    marked.

Never write
with pencil,
m'ija.
Write with ink
    or mud,
or berries grown in
gardens never owned,
  or, sometimes,
    if necessary,
      blood.

IV

Poems from *Sonnets and Salsa* (2001)

THe STOrYKeePer

Instructions from an historian

In the *jarros*, she says,
Look in the *jarros*.
The ones forgotten or shoved aside,
with a broken clay lip and color dulled by years
of hard use
and unmeditated abuse.

Search between the folds of rags,
the places no one else would look.
Often they are there, hiding.

Look in the garage,
in the dark corners.
Sometimes they are undiscovered, silent,
in the *tecorucho* sheds out back
or dumped in the alley,
wiped away from our lives, for the trash to take.
Others, hoarded like treasures the holder fears to reveal,
wrapped in a homemade *colcha*, in a wooden box
under the bed.
In the *viejitos'* eyes, in the twilight of death,
you read their secret, the eyes point you to the spot, stamp
"Remember" on the almost-forgotten box, and plead with you
to be the keeper
of the story.
To open the box, unwrap the *colcha* carefully,
save the scrawled story
protect it
as best you can.

Look in the places where ink does not show.
In the breaking voice
between the lines of a song.

Our history
is written in that song,
written on the voice,
sometimes written
on the heart.

Look at the hands.
The way the woman crosses herself when she passes
a certain field.
Everyone knows the story
of what happened there
late that night ninety years ago.
Everyone knows,
but it is not written.
The paragraphs of dangling bodies were too long, too ugly
to be written,
The sentences, like unfinished lives, too short
to make sense,
The letters of the words spelled out, distorted,
incomprehensible,
like mutilation of body parts
that started out in *belleza* and truth.

Look at the way she holds the *masa*, with both hands,
protecting, feeling its warmth,
memorizing the moment, for just a second,
before it's split apart,
into many *tortillas*
each to go their own way, some consumed rapidly,
some wasted, some disappeared,
never to be seen again.
In her gestures, her hesitations, her sigh of mourning
lie our history.

Ask the whispers, she whispers,
breathed out in unguarded moments,
when the soul is too tired to think,
the body too worn down to hurt more,
in the numbness of the night,

when the father wrestles with the unwritten history,
pleading to save it, speak it, bury it,
staring at the *pluma* across the room,
avoiding the paper.

Singing the Indian chant of a story
he will not tell his children
yet:
"They are too young.
Only 10.
Or 16.
Or 36.
Wait, wait—
I fear for them to know
what those hate-filled others
did to my grandfather.
They are too young.
Perhaps I too at only 60
am too young
to know,
too old
to forget."

Ask the whispers, she chants, Learn the chant.
Sing it slow and privately
like he does.
A sacred song
to be sung at only
sacred moments.

Look in the footwells of our steps,
the tablecorners rubbed smooth,
the marks on the walls where we have lived,
the fine and tired stitches in the clothing sewed and mended,
the careful fold of the shuck on the *tamal*,

the thumbprint curves of crepe paper flowers
trying to make *"Canta"* out of *"Llores."*

Learn to read the eyes, the hands, the spine.
You must be like a detective, or a spy.
Subtle, unnoticed, unrelenting.
For they are out there.
Our stories.
To be read in the tracks of tears now made
into wrinkles on the face,
in the scars we carry with pride,
in the grocery list marked with crayon on a junk mail
funeral home advertisement, in the Western Union
telegrams of money sent home to México,
in the eviction notices sent people whose address
has stayed the same for one hundred and fifty years.
You must be persistent, courageous. Go quickly. Urgently.
Go into the dark corners.
Unveil our treasures from the attic.
Go find it, hear it, touch it, write it down.

This is how
we keep
our
history.
This is how
we also
keep
our
soul.

EL Mercado/ Farmer's Market

-*¡Molcajetes!*
All ready to be cured
with little grains of rice.
Velvet Pictures!
For your living room, Señora—
Just look at this magnificent tiger here, or here—
Jesús, with his crown of thorns,
Or President Kennedy
(he was so good to us Mexicanos)
Get it for your comadre—the one that's so involved
in las neighborhood meetings!

"EXCUSE ME—DO YOU HAVE SOM-BRAY-ROES?
THOSE GREAT BIG ONES, YOU KNOW?"

-*¡Chiles!*
Fresh, hot, (and at a good price)
¡Chile Petín! ¡Serranos! ¡Jalapeños!
¡Chile Colorado, all ground up already!

"EXCUSE ME—ARE THESE HOT?"

—It feels so hot already. It's bugging me.
My father used to call these days
La Canícula, the Dog Days.

—Y *La Tencha*? Why isn't she here today?
Did she miss her ride?

—Oh, you didn't hear? Eeeee—what a tragedy!
Well, it's that her brother—the one that lives with her—
went to the Social Security office
so he could get paid his retirement,
and that they can't pay him, they say, because his boss
hadn't taken out anything for Social Security
after 40 years.

And that his chest is hurting him
And that his chest is hurting him
but he doesn't want to go to the doctor
because he doesn't have the with-what, you know?
And he's still not sixty-five
for Medicare—
so he just kept quiet and took it,
and didn't complain no more

"IS IT FAR FROM HERE TO THE ALAMO?"

—And that yesterday when Tencha gets home
with that big ole mountain of paper flowers in her arms,
the ones she sells, you know, and that the gringos
like so much,
well, on getting inside the door,
loaded down with everything and not seeing what was there,
that she stumbles on the body of her brother
on the floor, and she falls on top of him
flowers and all.
And the poor guy deader'n a . . .
Well! That La Tencha feels like dying of *pena*
que why didn't she make him go to the doctor
and pay it for him,
in little down payments or something,
like the lay-a-way at the stores, or *algo*,
all feelin bad, poor thing.
What a shame, hombre.

—Yeah, poor Tencha.
Listen, if you go by her house,
bring me the flowers and whatever she has to sell,
and I'll sell them for her here,
so the poor thing has for her expenses.

—Okay, Mano. And the corn and the fruit
That I don't sell today,
I'll take it to her—
After all, que tomorrow is another load.

—Yeah, tomorrow is another load.
—Así es la vida.

—Yeah, that's life.

-¡Molcajetes!
All ready to be cured
with little grains of rice,
Señora.

we never die

We never die.
We go through the trees in sunlight
hoping to be seen.
We never die.
We amass ourselves in sand dunes
awaiting patiently
the one who will record
our song.
We never die.
We take the wind's breath
and breathe it slowly
with all the living
with all those who loved
each in any way
the leaf bending to her branch
the moon covering her earth asleep
with the warm worn coverlet
of her long black hair
the unborn child dancing grateful
to the pulse
of his symphony-womb chamber
and me
drawn to the light in your eyes
that speaks colors of winter trees,
new-world skies,
dancing pearl-fetus, and sunrise
seen through the eyes
of the sand.

V

Poems from *Rebozos* (2012)

MUJERES DEL REBOZO ROJO

Who are we
las mujeres del rebozo rojo
who are always waiting for the light
hungry for the pink drops of morning
on the night's sky
searching for the sparkle of creation
of beginning
of life
on the dawn's edge
trying so hard
to open our eyes

Who are we
las mujeres del rebozo rojo
to want to reach and stretch and spread
and grow beyond our limits
yawning
pulling up our heads
pushing out our lungs
arching out our arms
resting only when in growth
transition
transformation
wanting only to be and
to become

to unfold our lives as if they were
rebozos
  revealing
    our inner colors
      the richness of our texture
          the strength of our weave
          the history of our making
  opening to
    all our fullness
      blossoms set free
  spreading our wings to the reach of the sky
    and awakening
      to who
        we really
          are

These Tacos

These *taquitos* que traigo
I made for you
for your mouth
whose taste I know so well
I know your belly too
and your hungers
your sighs and your desires
the rhythm of your chest
the softness of your breath
the way you burn me with your gaze
fill me with the heat of your skin
Tus ojos medio cerrados
mis labios medio abiertos
my shivering spine, your hands
mis suspiros, your
mouth
whose taste
I know so well

In these taquitos, the meat
is chopped small
and soft
for that missing tooth of yours
They're stuffed with *tomates*
sprinkled with cilantro
covered with *chile* that bites
Un besito de sal
lemon drizzled like summer rain
and always add plenty of beans.
These taquitos
I made for you
for your mouth
whose taste
I know
so well

curandera, your voice

Like a low *mesquite*-breeze
whistles softly through half a lung
and crackles like dried leaves in ancient bottles
Patient teas, potent herbs stand ready
in dusty jars along your kitchen shelves
and in the crowded cabinets of your well-aged
mind, where *remedios* older than mountains
overlap histories with miracles
and love with labor

Your memory leaves not one space to waste
or out of grace, but leads the lemon rinds, *comino* seeds,
reborn in dessicated age
as they grow to their purpose, stronger now
and *ojos de venado* add the haunting tenderness
of deer, the power of justice

Half-blind eyes whisper prayers through rippled light
sift sunshine through the sounds of centuries
Shuffling slippers pause
Barking dogs bow quiet for this Mass

Aglow with blessing
your hands exceed
the boundaries of their bones
and reach
to make
the cure

VI
Poems from *This River Here* (2015)

FEEDING YOU

I have slipped *chile* under your skin
    secretly wrapped in each *enchilada*
    hot and soothing,
    carefully cut into bitefuls for you as a toddler
    increasing in power and intensity as you grew
    until it could burn
    forever

    silently spiced into the rice
    soaked into the bean *caldo*
    smoothed into the avocado

    I have slipped *chile* under your skin
    drop by fiery drop
    until it ignited
    the sunaltar fire
    in your blood

I have squeezed *cilantro* into the breast milk
    made sure you were nurtured with the taste
    of green life and corn stalks
    with the wildness of thick leaves
    of untamed *monte*
    of unscheduled growth

I have ground the earth of these *Américas* in my *molcajete*
    until it became a fine and piquant spice
    sprinkled it surely into each spoonful of food
    that would have to expand to fit your soul

Dear Son
Dear Corn *Chile Cilantro* Son
This
is your *herencia*

This
is what is yours
This
    is what your mother fed you
    to keep you
    alive

BOTH SIDES OF THE BORDER

that deep delicious desire to run on two tracks   at the same time, jump back
and forth or let one foot fall inside each track,   like a little girl straddle-
skipping   two
sides   of a curb
to read the subtitles   in Spanish and
hear the English words   simultaneously
to write one   story in the
legal lines of the legal pad   and then to escape and scribble illegal
notes up the margin on a whole different   page
or poem   or poema.

I was born bilingual-   a lullaby between the
              Tex and the   Mex
My first nickname was an admonition   to a tío, primo hermano de mi papá,
as he painted the walls of my house   perched high on a ladder
I stood between the two   legs
Man Caes, I shouted,   a name I'd call him forever after, and he me
our bond, our new language   never as correct as expected
Never *Te vas a caer, hombre*   or even, *You're gonna fall, man!*
But even then I loved the   octopus arms of my mother language
              Tex-   Mex
even then I could not   stay within the required lines
not jump the border   not quite *step on a crack, break your mother's back*
not live on both   sides
of the border

to be deste lado y   dese lado
to straddle   the concrete curb
one foot falling on this side   next foot falling on the other
but more fun when I   rode the curb, balancing
above the world of   territories
owned   laughing in my

freedom   from either
and both

we were free   from *México*
not even bound   by their laws
but to prove we were not   conquered property of the US
we sassily insisted on still   saying "La Capital"
not for Washington DC   but for Mexico City.

My tongue runs to jump the language boundaries   sampling like a
gleefully wild child, of the goodies spread out   on both tables
all stuffed into the mouth at once by fingers   no forks, no limits, no portions
all impulse   *You can run, you can get away—*
The viejita watching the desserts   *can't catch you*
You are sin verguenza,   *high and high-powered*
wound up with the freeness   *sin zapatos*
without   *límites*

I write two   novels at the same time
I take two   languages, savor them with no restrictions
no one   measuring portions.
I stuff myself   with tasty words of
opposing   origins
I laugh, am unbroken   the donkey who still rears up
on hind legs to jump over the log   instead of lifting
one leg at a time, ladylike, to be gentle   for passengers
No, forget your hats, hang on to your seats   the ride is wild, it's
not guaranteed, it's not even defined   You don't know which
of the two dictionaries   to use
Like life and death, it gets all   tangled together
Maybe you're hearing me talk   maybe you're hearing yourself
maybe I answered a question   maybe I gave two different answers
like, which religion am I?   *Well, kind of Catholic, pero sin papeles*
since I was born and baptized   *a barrio Protestant.* Well okay, you say,
let's write down Christian   that ought to define it.

Well, no, I say, like what I   *am mainly is*
Native American   *Guadalupana*
you frown at   begin to study
the framed picture on   my wall of the darkskinned Virgin of
Guadalupe, alias   Aztec goddess Tonantzin

Um, also mixed with   *Sephardic Jew.*
You check for   papers.
No, I explain   *all unofficial, of course.*
I'm a mojada.   *I don't got papers.*

But I do got citizenship   two of 'm.
Like I got ownership.   Without the deeds.
These places are mine.   These spaces are mine.
These borders are mine.   Both sides of the river.
It's not that I don't belong. It's just that I
belong twice.   Don't we all?

It is time.   It is more than twice past the time.
I want an altar.   No, two.
One will be an
Altar to Lupe, the   pregnant
virgin   (Well, most things *are*
medically possible   aren't they?)
The Catholic Holy Mother with unborn mestizo baby—yes, openly PG
Wearing her black belt   the Aztec sign of pregnancy
Brown Indian face,
Moon, Sun, Gold Stars in cloak   Red dress, Black belt of
Pregnancy, identical to   the Aztec Goddess Tonatzin.
A Spanish plot?   To convert Indians to Catholicism?
No, an Indian plot   To convert Catholicism to Indians.
Subversively they called her   Queen of the Americas,
Her only Crown the   Indian Sun, simultaneous with a
Footstool Moon,   her hands folded humbly, no one's fooled.
I'll keep her big bright   Mexican Colors, Green and red with gold stars

But maybe I'll add   something (Blue jeans? Dreamcatcher earrings?
Green card?)   Maybe not.

We pray to her   She prays to someone else, maybe to us?
Please, Virgencita . . .   Please, non-Virgencitos . . .
Protect us we say   Attack, she says, Charge ahead for yourselves.

The other box   drawer, altar
becomes a   Dia de los Muertos.
I'll call it   All My Children, like the soap opera, with the
ad from the   soap opera pasted behind it
and pictures   of all my kids, even the ones who weren't
born.   Children, the very sprouting of
life   but in the middle of Dia de los Muertos, the very sprouting of
death   And like in every Day of the Dead altar, everyone in it will be
a muertito   a little laughing skeleton.
So there will be my kids,   all of 'm
The live muertitos   and the dead muertitos.
All with sweatsuits from   Old Navy, or Ross, or the Dollar Store
in different colors   and their initial on it
And also *mis*   books and ideas and ancestors, and a bunch of other
people   who aren't my children but
could've been   and a globe of
the world.

Drawers   altares
in my home   two, so you never get too serious about
just one   never get too committed to
one ideology   one language
one focus   one religión.
My bicultural   bi-altares
one to an Aztec   Christian
pregnant   virgin. And one to
all the dead we've   loved before

Hung together, to life   and to death
Or is it, to death   and to life. Or is it,
both things   at the same time
in both   places
always both sides   of every
          border

THere've always Been raTTlesnakes,

especially if you live in Texas,
quietly coiled potent surprises
filled with regrettable poisons
scorpions startled under rocks
tails poised for incisive action
flash floods submerging the floor, the bed
wiping away anything not rooted yards deep
droughts that wilt the cactus,
bake the trees, suck dry the elderly

there've always been rattlesnakes,
husbands collapsed to the ground,
stores gone broke
grandmothers fading away,
bills eating the grocery money,
heart attacks at midnight,
heat strokes at 4 p.m.
wagons, cars, bikes,
crumpled into broken skeletons
tornados that wreak havoc,
lightning that incinerates homes
cancers that appear when least expected,
disasters that life or human or nature makes

But even the cruelly unexpected
fangs of rattlesnakes
grow brittle over time
crumble into the offended earth
even droughts bathe eventually
in the abundant August chubascos
even long-staring skeletons
become rich abono
fertilizing the persistent pecan trees
    the hope-filled shoots of Chile Serrano
    the motivation of survivors trying to rebuild
        bone by desperate bone
        to rebuild

survival instructions, summer, 103 degrees

Feel yourself sizzle on the streets
Sizzle on the streets
Sashay sassy as salsa
Slip survival into sunglare like a native
Toughen up the soles
Strengthen the heart muscle
Reinforce the mind with steel and sunrise
Drink more water
Bless the air conditioner
Fry your *huevos rancheros* on the sidewalk
Attend the wake
Give a dollar to the homeless man on the corner
Holding his bright blue windshield-cleaner-spraybottle
wiping circles in the empty air
Hoping for a yes
some coins
a bed
Lasso the chaos of your collapsing life like a lost steer
Wrangle it with this well-worn rope
made to survive the torrid heat
the chaparral of baked dirt
the creeping cancer of years peeled to bone
Feel yourself sizzle on the streets
Sizzle on the streets
Sashay
sassy as salsa

THIS RIVER HERE

This river here
is full of me and mine.
This river here
is full of you and yours.

Right here
(or maybe a little farther down)
My great-grandmother washed the dirt
out of her family's clothes,
soaking them, scrubbing them,
bringing them up
clean.

Right here
(or maybe a little farther down)
My grampa washed the sins
out of his congregation's souls,
baptizing them, scrubbing them,
bringing them up
clean.

Right here
(or maybe a little farther down)
My great-great grandma froze with fear
as she glimpsed,
between the lean, dark trees,
a lean, dark Indian peering at her.
She ran home screaming, "¡Ay, los Indios!
Aí vienen los I-i-indios!!"
as he threw pebbles at her,
laughing.
Till one day she got mad
and stayed
and threw pebbles
right back at him!

After they got married,
they built their house right here
(or maybe a little farther down.)

Right here,
my father gathered
mesquite beans and wild berries
working with a passion
during the Depression.
His eager sweat poured off
and mixed so easily
with the water of this river here.

Right here,
my mother cried in silence,
so far from her home,
sitting with her one brown suitcase,
a traveled trunk packed full with blessings,
and rolling tears of loneliness and longing
which mixed (again so easily)
with the currents of this river here.

Right here we'd pour out picnics,
and childhood's blood from
dirty scrapes on dirty knees,
and every generation's first-hand stories
of the weeping lady La Llorona
haunting the river every night,
crying "Ayyy, mis hi-i-i-ijos!"—
(It happened right here!)

The fear dripped off our skin
and the blood dripped off our scrapes
and they mixed with the river water,
right here.

Right here,
the stories and the stillness

of those gone before us
haunt us still,
now grown, our scrapes in different places,
the voices of those now dead
quieter,
but not too far away

Right here we were married,
you and I,
and the music filled the air,
danced in,
dipped in,
mixed in
with the river water.

   dirt and sins,
   fear and anger,
   sweat and tears, love, music,
   Blood.
   And memories
It was right here!

And right here we stand,
washing clean our memories,
baptizing our hearts,
gathering past and present,
dancing to the flow
we find
right here
or maybe—
a little farther
down.

ACKNOWLEDGMENTS

I would like to thank my editors, my publishers, my friends, family, and those who believed in me throughout this long, non-standard and non-recommended route to becoming a committed writer. I am especially grateful to la gente del barrio, la gente del pasado, y la gente who struggle daily and with faith and stubbornness to survive: you have been my inspiration and my teachers. My best lines have come from your lives.

The first books of poetry that I published were because of courageous and independent-thinking publishers, some of them garage-presses, kitchen presses, Mom-and-Pop presses, who saw a need to make diverse voices available to the readers of this world, and took valiant and visionary action, dedicating their lives to this process. They include (but are not limited to) Cecilio García-Camarillo and Reyes Cárdenas (Caracol, Rifán Press, Magazín...); Angela de Hoyos and Moises Sandoval (M&A Editions); Ernesto Padilla (Lalo Press, Santa Monica Press); and Bryce Milligan (Wings Press). If anyone has been responsible for my freedom and productiveness, it has been you. The poems in all of the sections except the first were printed in your pages, and in books that other, larger presses were scared to publish because they included too much Spanish, themes that were too Chicano, or ideas that were before their time. You were unafraid, unapologetic, and amazing.

While many of these poems have been published in journals, magazines, and anthologies throughout the world, I have not listed all of these (to avoid boredom) but have indicated only the complete books in which they appear. Still, I remember with great fondness the Mexico City magazine, Blanco Movil;

the 1984 Scott-Foresman American Literature textbook; the New Zealand anthology from the Wellington International Poetry Festival; the anthology published in Calcutta, India, Yapanchitra: A Portrait of life; the tiny, stapled 1970s Chicano Lit series, Tejidos; the East Coast private school yearbook; and all the other odd places in which they appeared. For poems that have been published in more than thirty places, like "marked," "allí por la calle san luis," and "This River Here," thank you to all the places worldwide committed to publishing literature and the arts, from *Caracol* in 1975 to the *Texas Observer* in the 1980s to the Yale School of Divinity's journal *Reflections* in 2013. As for the new poems in Section One, their acknowledgments for first publication are listed below.

In closing, I must thank my closest and my dearest team-members, those who supported me emotionally all these years, and who, within a quick twenty-one-month period, all three ceased to walk this earth (in physical form anyway) but never fully left me —my mother, who bought me from her meager coins Volume 1 of the *Childcraft Encyclopedia*, entitled *Children's Rhymes and Verses* and who encouraged me in my dreams to get an education, betting on me when the others bet against me; my "Baby Brother," who always cheered on his baby sister and her dreams; and my beloved husband, who never for a minute doubted I could be the writer I longed to be, who listened to all the crazy ideas, and read all the drafts with the same enthusiasm. You three are the reason I am here, y los quiero en todo momento y para siempre.

Carmen Tafolla, 2018

First Publication of Poems in the New Poems Section:

"It was so Cold" and "Gently Apart": *New Verse News*, 2009.
"This is a Place": *Langdon Review of the Arts*, 2014.
"Something Severed: Entre Guadalupe y Malinche": *Tejanas in Literature & Art*, University of Texas Press, 2015.

"Where My Father Built His House": *Langdon Review of the Arts*, 2014.

"What to do while Awaiting the Angel of Death": *San Antonio Express-News*, April 9, 2017.

ABOUT THE AUTHOR

Dr. Carmen Tafolla is the author of more than thirty books, seven screenplays, and more than two hundred short stories, poems, and articles in journals, magazines, and college and high school textbooks, Kindergarten "Big Books," and even city buses. Called by Rigoberto Gonzales "the Zora Neale Hurston of the Chicano Community," Tafolla has performed her one-woman theatrical show in England, Spain, Germany, Norway, Ireland, Canada, Mexico, New Zealand, and throughout the US. Tafolla is a professor of transformative children's literature at the University of Texas San Antonio. Her works are archived in the Nettie Lee Benson Collection at the University of Texas Austin. She collects jarros, oil cans, and wooden boxes, and lives in San Antonio with her daughter.